Hands-On Projects

WILD WEST

Active Learning about Pioneers

by Carol Wawrychuk & Cherie McSweeney
illustrated by Philip Chalk

Contents

Entire contents copyright ©1999 by Monday Morning Books, Inc.
For a complete catalog, please write to the address below:
P.O. Box 1680, Palo Alto, CA 94302 U.S.A.
Call us at: 1-800-255-6049
E-mail us at: MMBooks@aol.com
Visit our Web site: http://www.mondaymorningbooks.com

Monday Morning Books is a registered trademark of Monday Morning Books, Inc.

Permission is hereby granted to reproduce student materials in this book for
non-commercial individual or classroom use.
ISBN 1-57612-073-2
Printed in the United States of America
987654321

Introduction

Wagons ho! Circle around the campfire! The past comes alive when children create their own covered wagon from a large appliance box and old sheets. Children fashion a miner's visor to wear while they pan for gold. They enjoy living in a one-room log cabin fashioned from dryer boxes. Cooking has never been so much fun as over a campfire ring fashioned from paper lunch bags, paper towel tubes, and tissue paper. There is even a hanging pot made from an empty ice cream container! For added fun, teach the children campfire songs to sing around the campfire ring.

The *Wild West* theme unit is the perfect opportunity to discuss historical changes with the children. Explain that before people drove cars, they rode in covered wagons and stagecoaches. Lead discussions about why cooking might have been done over a campfire instead of a stove. On a map of the United States, show children where the west is and trace the routes pioneers used when traveling across the country.

In several activities, children mix two colors of paint to make a new color. Discuss this concept before children embark on the activity. Ask the children what other colors can be mixed together to form a different color. Let them experiment! Other activities in this book reinforce children's ability to recognize colors and color words and to match numbers.

Children's curiosity will lead them to many exciting adventures in the wide-open spaces of the Wild West!

Helpful Hints:
• Stores often will give away their used boxes.
• Boxes can collapse for easy transporting and storing.
• Some boxes may be reused for different projects.
• Use cable ties, string, or yarn for assembling the box projects. (Cable ties provide the sturdiest form of attaching.)
• A mat knife or Exacto blade works best for cutting boxes, but a sharp kitchen knife will work well, too. Use the knife or blade well out of the way of children!
• Local businesses often will donate supplies.
• Shop discount stores for cotton balls, cotton swabs, sponges, and paper goods.
• Scour garage sales for miscellaneous items. such as wire whisks, potato mashers, and cookie cutters.
• Involve parents in your projects. They can save items for you.

Log Cabin

Materials:

Two dryer boxes, cardboard
tubes (from wrapping paper,
paper towels, or toilet tissue), tongue depressors or Popsicle sticks,
cable ties or string, tempera paint (brown, black, and white),
shallow tins for paint, blocks for stamp painting, paintbrushes or
rollers, marker, paste, scissors, sharp instrument for cutting (for
adult use only)

Directions:

1. Remove one end of one of the boxes. (Leave the other end intact.)
2. Cut a pitched roof shape on the front and back of the box.
3. Cut a door and a window in the box.

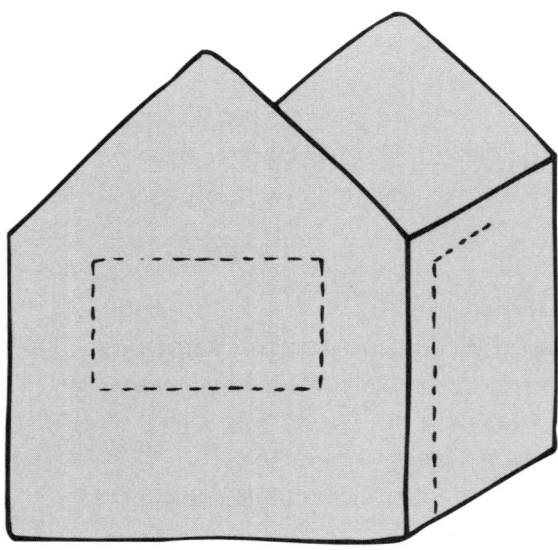

4. Cut a section of the second dryer box for the roof, and fold
it in half.

Log Cabin

5. Punch and align holes on the roof and the pitched roof-shaped box. Attach the roof to the cabin with cable ties. (Remove the loose ends of the cable ties.)

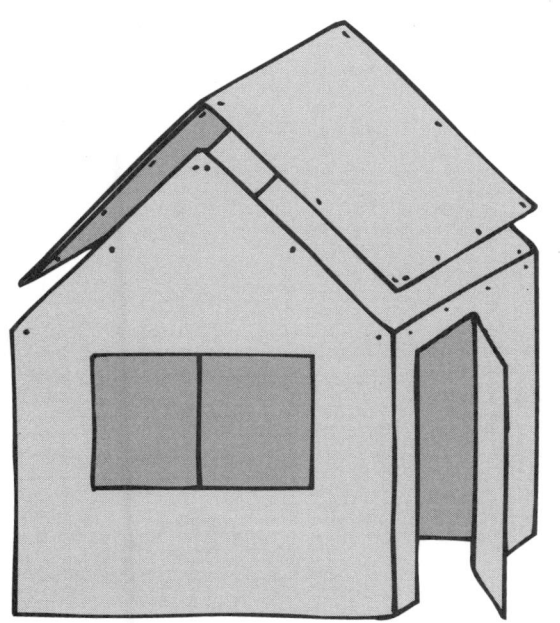 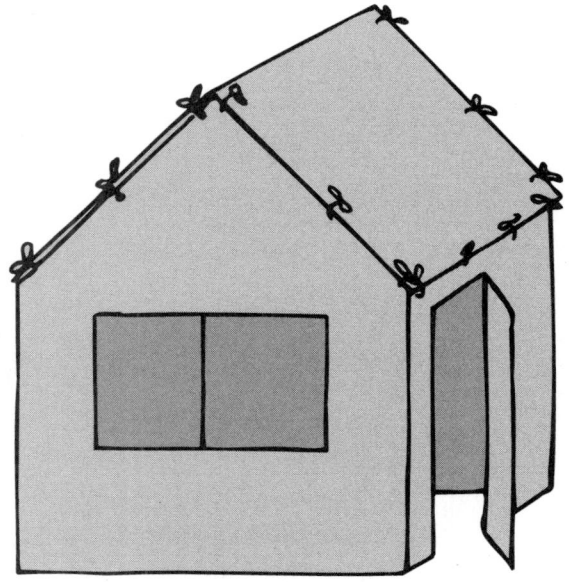

6. Cut a section from the second dryer box for the chimney. Punch and align four holes in the chimney and the back of the cabin.
7. Have the children mix black and white paint to make gray.
8. Place the chimney on a flat surface, and provide blocks for the children to use to stamp paint it.
9. Have the children paint the cabin and roof brown and tan. (They can make tan paint by mixing brown and white.)
10. Once the paint has dried, attach the chimney to the cabin with cable ties. (Cut off loose ends of the cable ties.)
11. Have the children paste cardboard tubes and tongue depressors to the cabin for the logs. (This will take a lot of paste!)

Facts to Share:
The pioneers used the resources around them to survive. Many frontier homes were built from rough cut trees.

Option:
• For a taller house, remove the top of the box, and use the cardboard to make a V-shaped roof. Put the roof on and secure the two sides.

Covered Wagon

Materials:

Refrigerator box, sturdy plastic garden border edging, white sheet (double bed size), black construction paper, cable ties, brown tempera paint, shallow tins for paint, paintbrushes or rollers, white crayon, glue, scissors, sharp instrument for cutting (for adult use only)

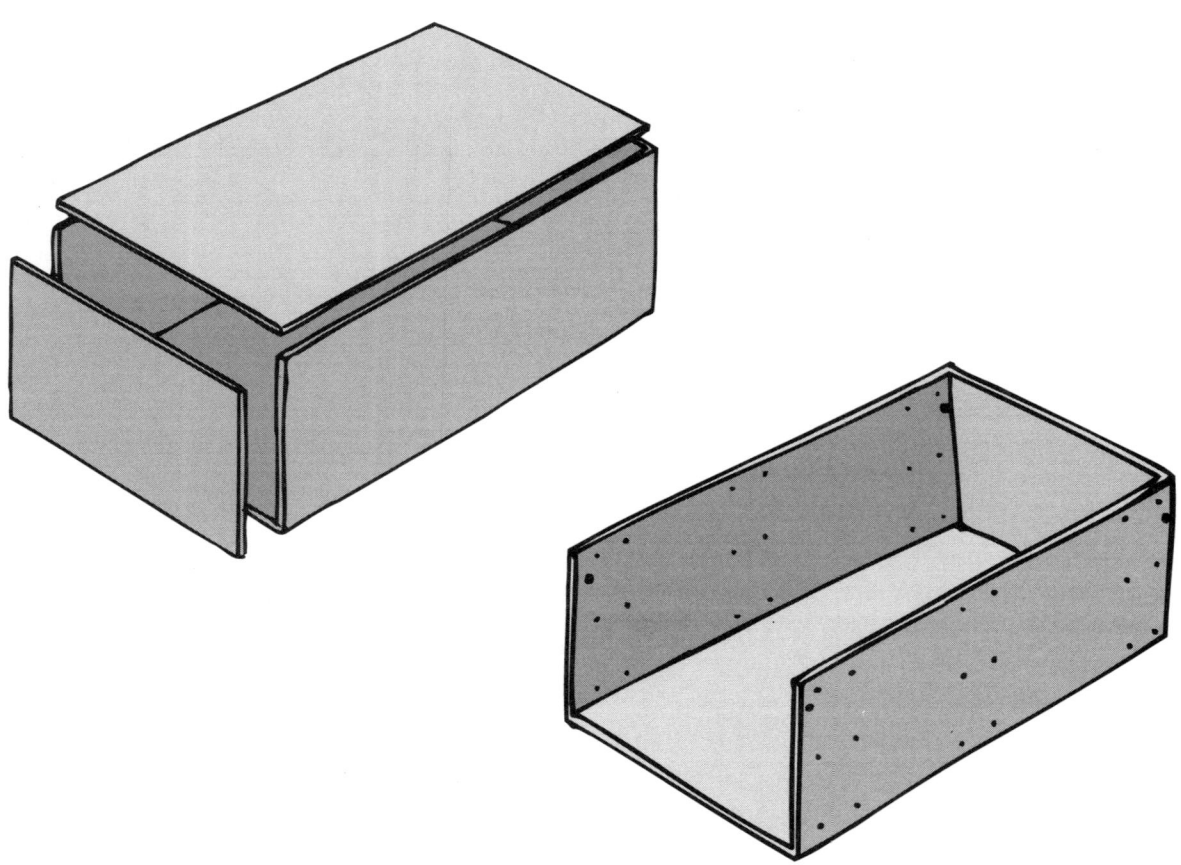

Directions:

1. Place the box on its side. Cut off one end and the top side of the box.

2. In each side of the box, cut two rows of three sets of holes directly across from one another. The distance between the slits should be slightly wider than the garden border.

Covered Wagon

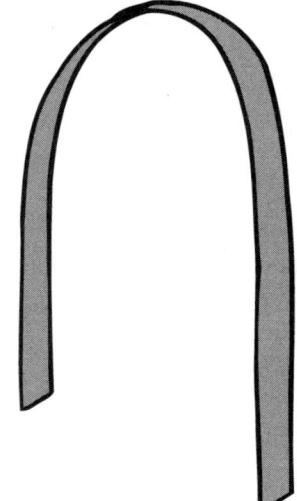

3. Cut three lengths of garden border edging to the desired height of the covered wagon.

4. Pull the cable ties through the slits with the loose ends on the inside of the box. Secure the garden border edging to the box with the cable ties. (Cut off the loose ends of the cable ties.) The garden border edging now forms an arch.

5. Use the white crayon to trace four large circles onto black construction paper. Let the children cut out these wagon wheels. (Spokes can be cut in the center of the wheels.) The wheels can also be painted on.

6. Have the children paint the box brown.

7. Once the paint has dried, cover the wagon with the sheet. To secure the sheet, poke four holes in the cardboard near the corners of the sheet. Poke the sheet through and knot it.

8. Have the children glue the paper wheels onto the wagon.

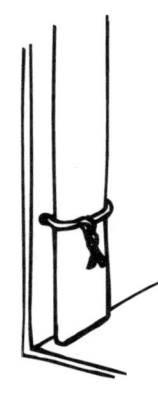

Facts to Share:
Many people traveled west in wagon trains. Entire families lived out of wagons covered with heavy cloth. These wagons transported furniture, household supplies, and food.

Option:
• Place large blocks or small chairs inside the wagon for seating.

Book Link:
• *Buffalo Thunder* by Patricia Wittman (Marshall Cavendish)

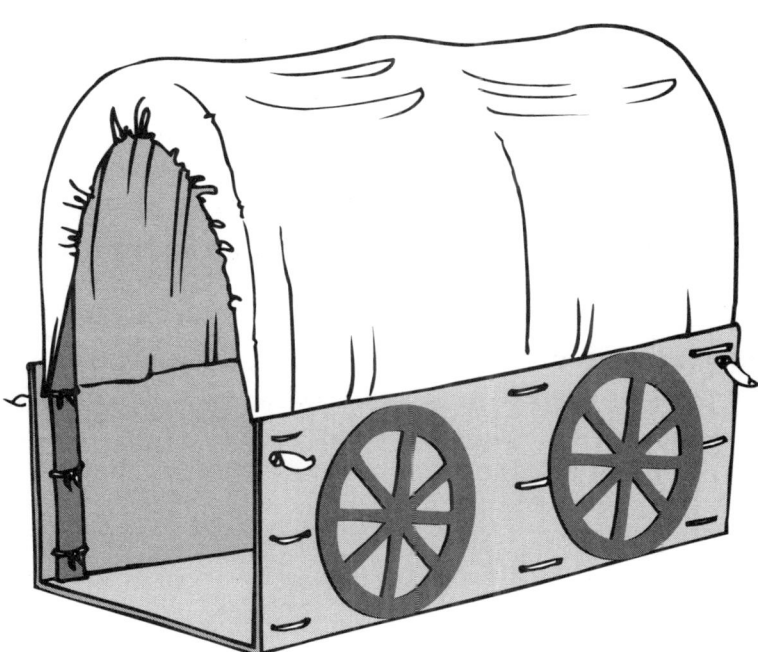

Wild West ©1999 Monday Morning Books, Inc.

Super Sawhorse

Materials:

Horse Head (p. 9), sawhorse, flat piece of cardboard, heavy string or yarn, jute or rope (black or brown), tempera paint (brown and white), shallow tins for paint, plastic scouring pads, marker, sharp instrument for cutting (for adult use only), saw (for adult use only), hammer and nails (for adult use only), glue, stapler

Directions:

1. Cut the sawhorse to a safe height for children to sit on it.
2. Enlarge and duplicate the Horse Head and cut it out.
3. On the flat piece of cardboard, trace the horse head pattern twice and cut out. Cut a notch in the neck to allow for the sawhorse legs. Punch holes down the back of the head. Make two holes under the chin.
4. Cut the jute or rope into 1-foot (30-cm) sections.
5. For the horse's mane, have the children tie the jute or rope through the holes.
6. Nail the horse heads on both sides of the sawhorse. Tie the horse heads together through the holes under the chin. (See pattern, p. 9.)
7. Cut out two versions of the ear pattern. Fold them in half lengthwise. Staple the flaps together at the bottom and attach to the horse's head with glue or staples.
8. Let the children mix brown and white paint to make tan.
9. Have the children use scouring pads to paint the horse. The horse can be painted two-tone, if desired.
10. Once the paint has dried, cut lengths of jute or rope and nail them to the rear of the horse for the tail.

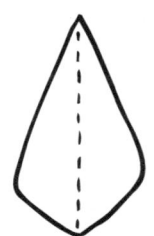

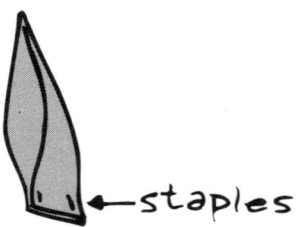

←staples

Horse Head

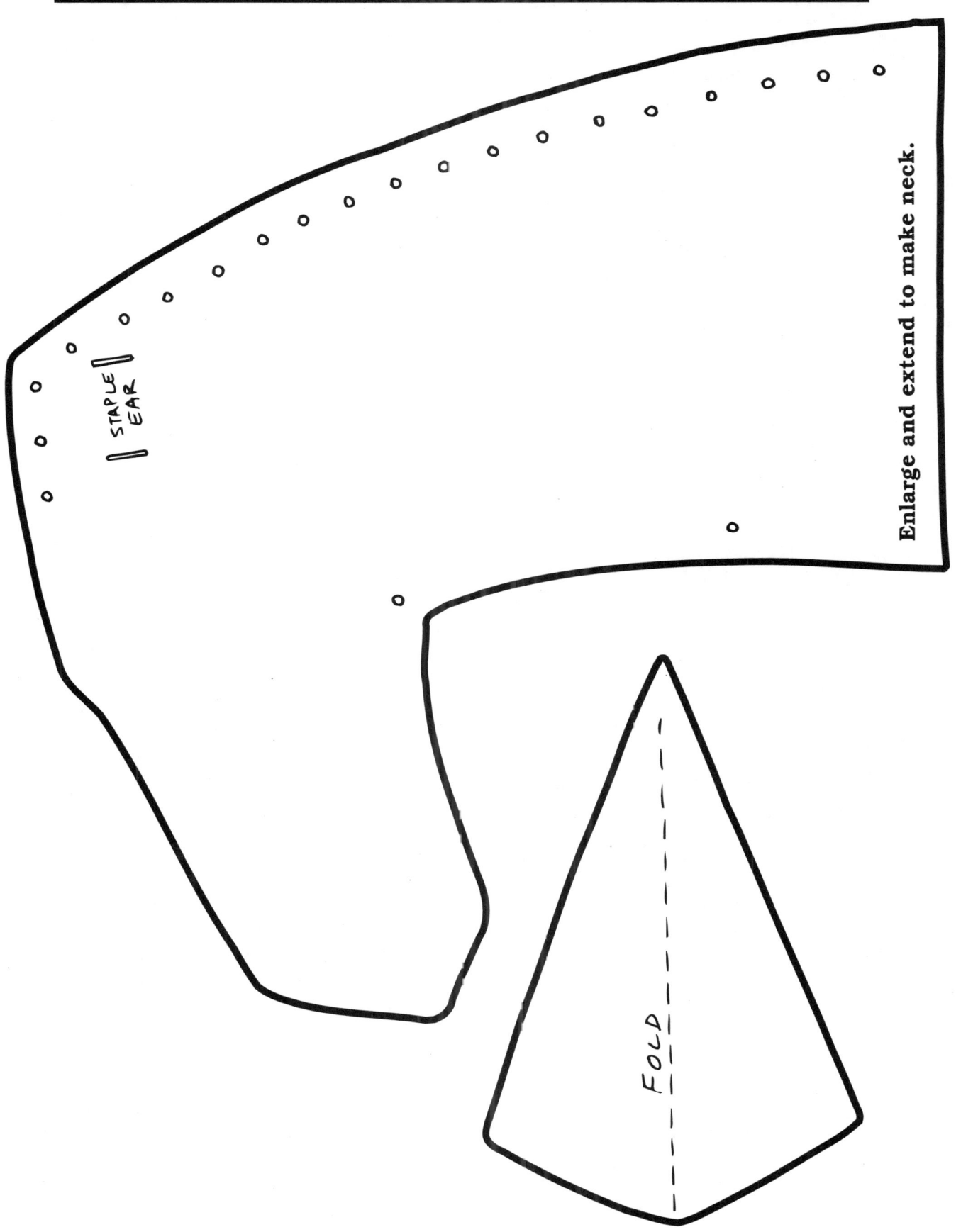

STAPLE EAR

Enlarge and extend to make neck.

FOLD

Saddlebags

Materials:
Burlap, cardboard, marker, yarn, yarn needles, scissors

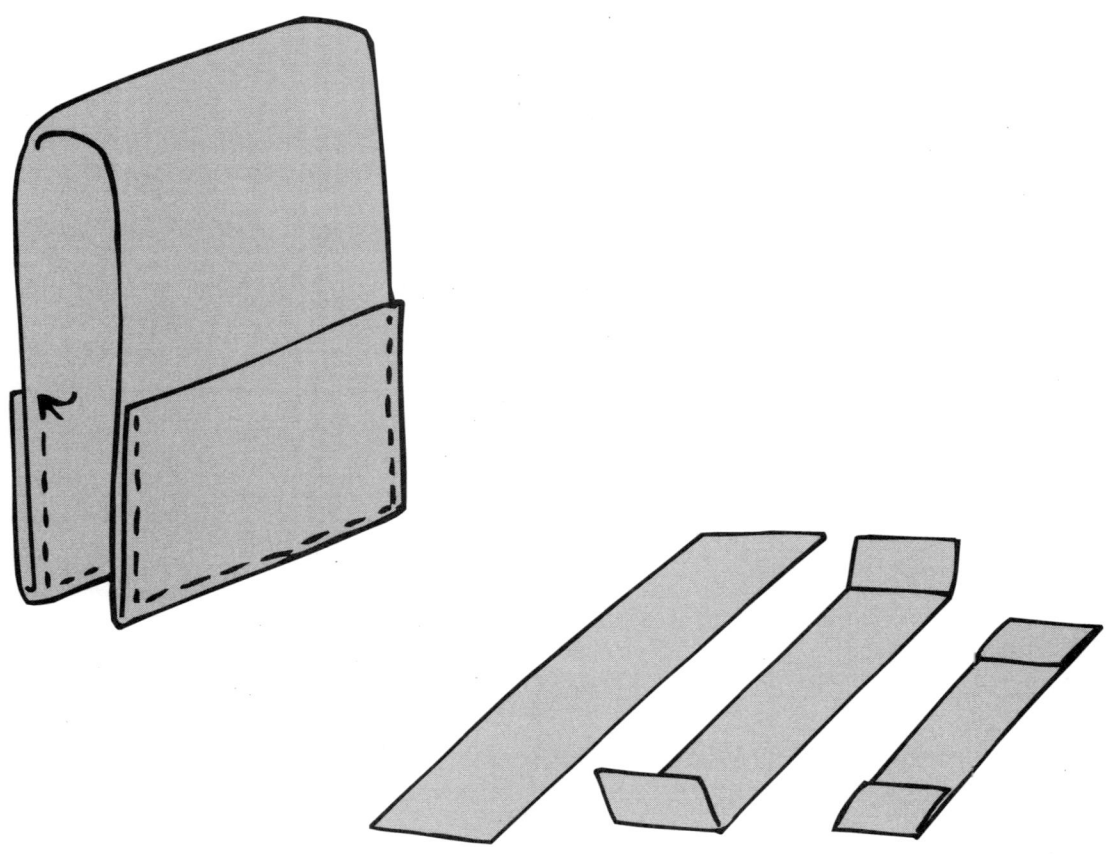

Directions:
1. On a piece of burlap, draw a long rectangle. Make one rectangle per child.
2. For each child, cut two pieces of cardboard slightly smaller than the width of the burlap.
3. On each saddlebag, place a piece of cardboard at each end of the piece of burlap and fold up the burlap to form pockets. (The cardboard keeps the children from stitching through the center of the pockets.)
4. For each pocket, knot a piece of yarn to a needle and to one end of the pocket.
5. Have the children stitch around the edge of the pockets.
6. Make a knot at the finished end and cut the needles free.

Note:
• Place the saddlebags over the Super Sawhorse (p. 8).

Pony Express Mail

Materials:

Burlap, cardboard, marker, yarn, yarn needles, stapler, scissors, white paper, small envelopes (one per child), crayons or markers

Directions:

1. Follow the directions for making a set of saddlebags (p. 10), but make the saddlebags extra large. The pockets should be large enough to hold several envelopes.
2. Pair up the children and explain that each child will be drawing a picture for his or her partner.
3. Have each child draw a picture on a piece of paper. The pictures should be about the Wild West. (You might want to read children books about the west first.)
4. Give each child a small envelope and have the children write their names on the envelopes. (Help those who need it.)
5. The partners should exchange the envelopes (so each child has an envelope that has his or her partner's name on it).
6. Have the children put the pictures into the envelopes.
7. Put several envelopes in the pockets on the large saddlebag.
8. Let children take turns being the pony express rider who delivers the mail. They can pull an envelope from the saddlebag and deliver it to the correct person. Help children who need it. Continue to fill the saddlebags with more envelopes as children work through them.

Note:

• Store the large saddlebag and the envelopes with the children's names in the classroom. Let children use these whenever they wish in their dramatic play.

Stagecoach

Materials:
Dryer box or refrigerator box (cut in half), black construction paper, tempera paint (red and black), shallow tins for paint, paintbrushes and rollers, marker, sharp instrument for cutting (for adult use only)

Directions:
1. Place the box with the closed end up.
2. On one side of the box, cut a door with a window and a hole for a handle. Cut several windows on each side of the box.
3. Trace four large circles on construction paper for the wheels.
4. Provide red paint for the children to use to paint the box sides. They can use the black paint to cover the roof and top edge.
5. Have the children cut out the four black circles. Help them cut out spokes.
6. Once the paint has dried, have the children glue the wheels to the stagecoach.
7. Write "Stagecoach" above the door.

Note:
• The driver can sit on a long hollow wooden block or small chair.

Option:
• Purchase colored tickets, or make tickets from colored construction paper. Let the children take turns being the passengers or driver of the stagecoach. The driver can collect the tickets at the start of the ride.

Facts to Share:
One form of transportation in the west, stagecoaches carried people and merchandise between major cities.

Socko the Riding Pony

Materials:
Socks (one per child), gift wrap tubes (one per child), newspaper, yarn, felt, clear packing tape or masking tape, colored markers, scissors

Directions:
1. Cut long pieces of yarn for the ponies' manes.
2. Cut felt into small triangles for the ponies' ears.
3. Have each child stuff the foot section of his or her sock with newspaper.
4. Let the children insert the gift wrap tubes into the socks and fasten with tape.
5. Have the children tape the yarn and felt to the socks.
6. Provide markers for the children to use to add facial features to their ponies.

Options:
• The children can glue on buttons for their ponies' eyes.
• Help the children paint facial features on the ponies with cotton swabs.
• Use colored masking tape to bind the socks to the tubes.

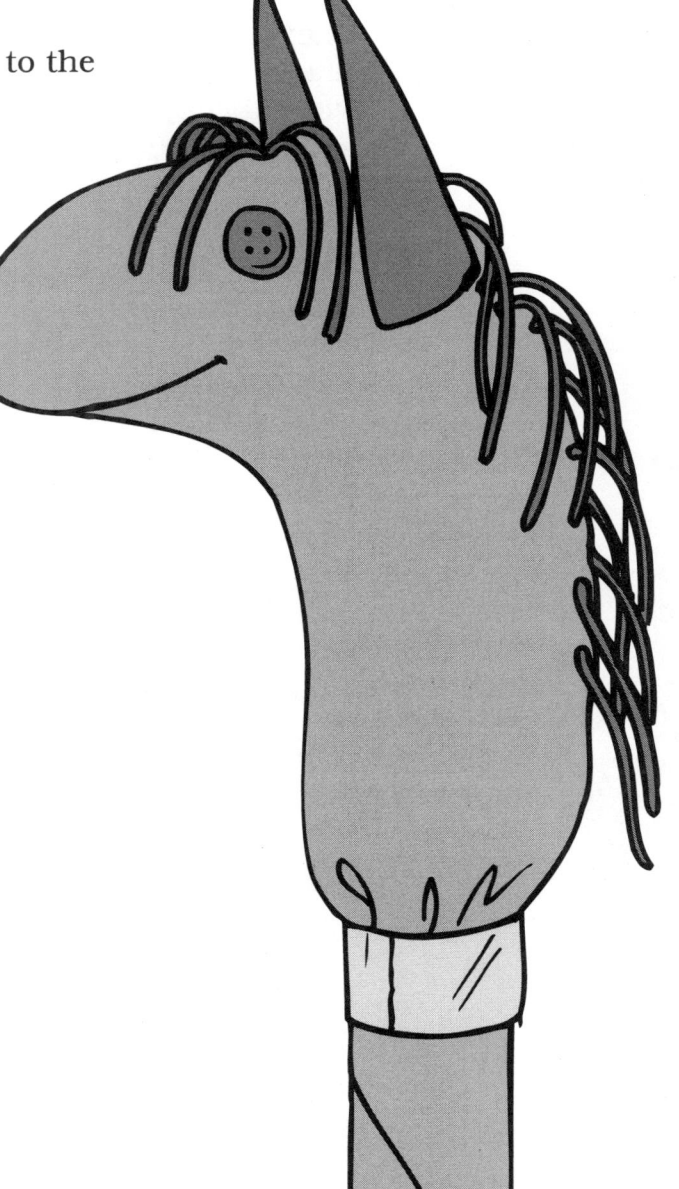

Sheriff's Badge

Materials:
Sheriff's Badge (this page), sturdy paper, safety pins (one per child), crayons and markers, colored pencils, hole punch, scissors

Directions:
1. Trace the Sheriff's Badge pattern onto sturdy paper, and cut it out. Make one per child.
2. On the badges, write the word "Sheriff" followed by a child's name—for example, "Sheriff Philip." Make a badge for each child.
3. Provide markers, crayons, and colored pencils for the children to use to decorate their badges.
4. Punch a hole in the top of each badge, and use a safety pin to secure the badge to the child's clothing.

Note:
• Older children may be able to cut out the badges themselves.

Wild West Wanted Poster

Materials:
Wanted Poster (p. 16), instant camera and film or crayons and markers, glue

Directions:
1. Explain that in the Wild West, wanted posters were put around towns to alert people about trouble makers. Explain that the children will be making their own posters, but that the posters will describe people who do good things, not bad things.
2. Make a copy of the Wanted Poster for each child.
3. Have the children dictate things that they do well. For example, a child might say, "I can ride my bike," or "I'm a good artist." Help children who need it. Prompt them with questions. Then write the statements on the children's posters.
4. Take a photo of each child and have the children glue the pictures on their posters. (If a camera is not available, children can draw self-portraits.)
5. Post the wanted posters in an area where the children can look at their own pictures and the pictures of their friends.

Option:
• Instead of using an instant camera, have parents send in photos of their children. Be sure to let them know that the photos will be used in an art project and should not be originals.

15   *Wild West* ©1999 Monday Morning Books, Inc.

NAME

KNOWN FOR: _____

_____

_____

Wild West Vest

Materials:

Butcher paper, yarn, clear packing tape or masking tape, tempera paint (in assorted colors), shallow tins for paint, gadgets for painting (wire whisk, cookie cutters, potato masher), marker, hole punch, scissors

Directions for One Vest:

1. Cut a vest shape out of butcher paper. Reinforce the edges with tape. Align and punch holes according to the diagram. Make one vest per child.
2. Provide tempera paint and assorted gadgets for children to use to stamp paint the vests.

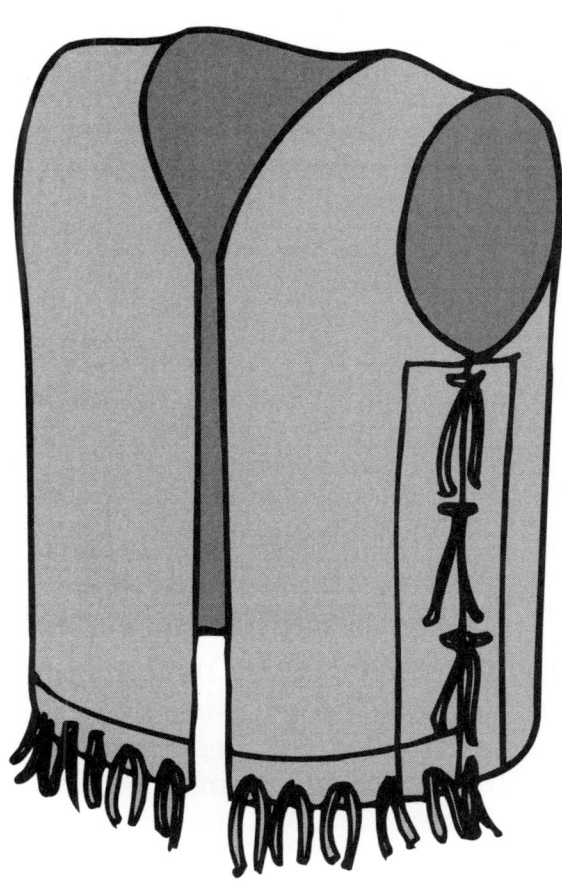

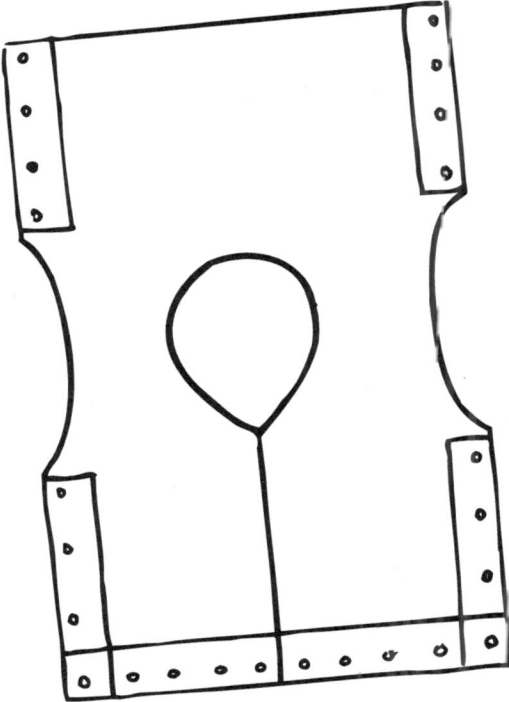

Wild West Vest

3. Once the paint has dried, fold the vest at the shoulders.

4. For each vest, cut ten pieces of yarn (approximately 1 ft/.3 m long) and two pieces of yarn long enough to lace up the sides of the vest.

5. Wrap a small piece of masking tape around one end of each long piece of yarn. (This will make it easier for children to thread the yarn through the holes.) Tie the other ends of the pieces of yarn to holes on each side of the vest.

6. Have the children loosely lace the sides of the vests. Tie the loose ends.

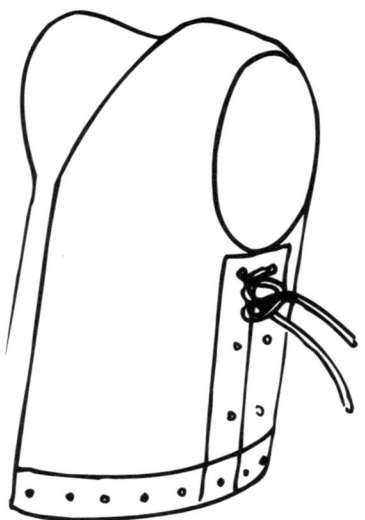 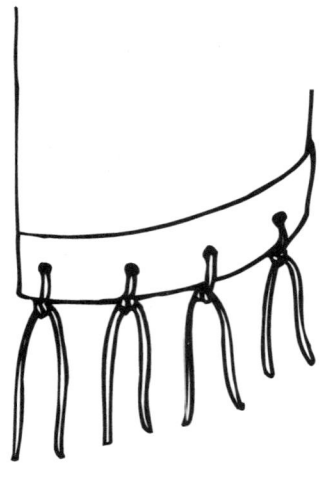

7. Children can use the other pieces of yarn to make loop knot fringe. Demonstrate how to fold the yarn in half, insert the loop of yarn through the hole, bring the two loose ends of yarn through the loop, and pull gently. Continue for each hole to complete the fringe.

Option;
• Children can "fringe" the sides of the vests, rather than lacing them (see above).

Book Link:
• *The Cowboy and the Black-Eyed Pea* by Tony Johnston and Warren Ludwig (Putnam)

Ten-Gallon Hat

Materials:
Hat Brim pattern (p. 20), paper bags (one per child; the bags should be large enough to sit on the top of a child's head), paper, poster board, brown felt or tissue paper, yarn, aluminum foil, glue, stapler or masking tape, scissors, marker, hole punch

Directions:
1. Make two copies of the Hat Brim pattern and cut them out. Tape the patterns together to make a large circle.
2. Enlarge the Hat Brim pattern so that the inner hole is big enough for a child's head.
3. Trace the pattern onto poster board and cut it out. Make one per child.
4. Use a marker to divide each paper bag in half, width-wise.
5. Have the children cut their bags in half.
6. Have the children open their bags. Help each child insert his or her open bag through the brim of the hat, then staple or tape the two together.
7. Children can glue felt or tissue pieces to their hat brims.
8. While the hats are drying, have the children make hatbands by rolling long strips of aluminum foil.
9. Once the brims are dry, children can wrap and twist the bands to the hats.
10. Punch a hole on opposite sides of each hat, and attach a piece of yarn to each hole. These yarn pieces will be tied under a child's chin to keep the hat on.

Book Link:
• *Boss of the Plains: The Hat That Won the West*
by Laurie Carlson (DK Publishing)

Note:
• If the paper bags are too small, make a small slit in the back and spread the bag to accommodate a child's head.

 Wild West ©1999 Monday Morning Books, Inc.

Hat Brim

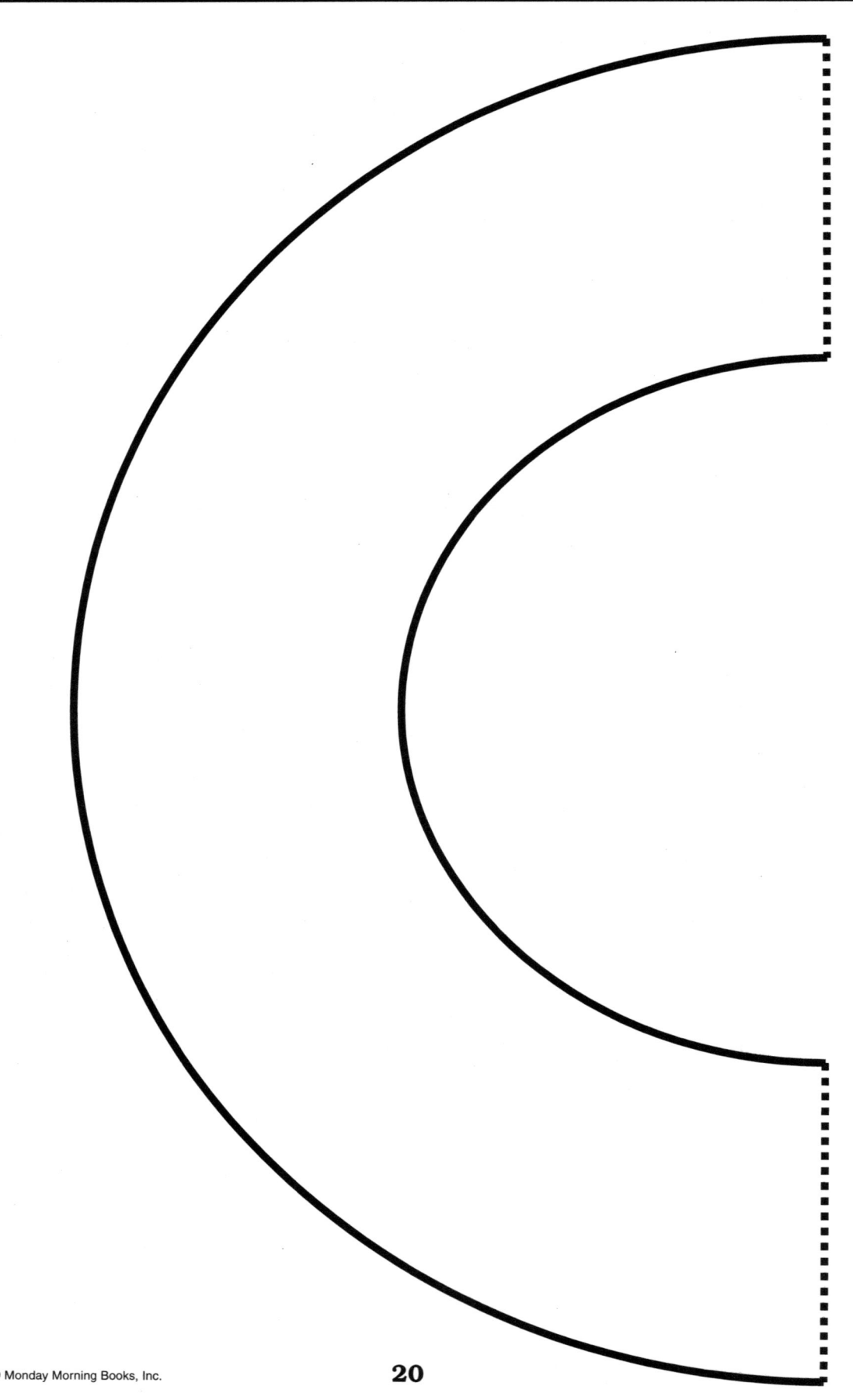

Riding Chaps

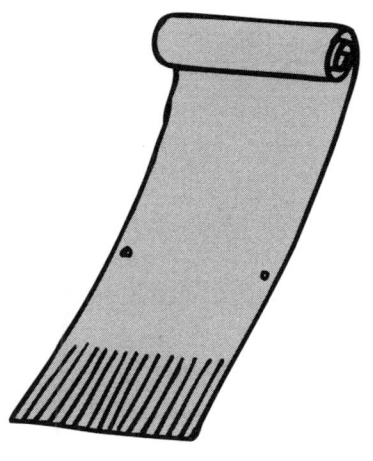 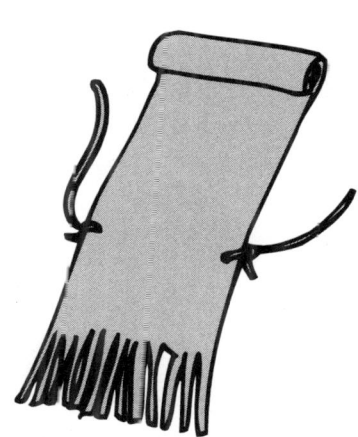 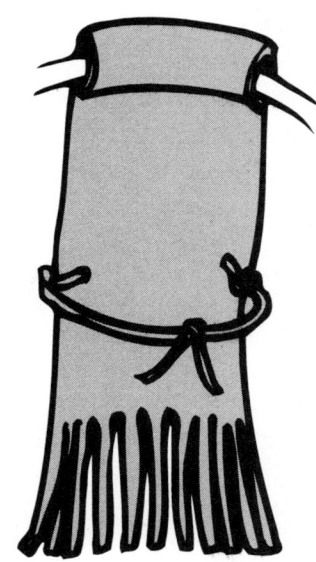

Materials:
Paper grocery bags (one per child), wide-band elastic, clear packing tape or masking tape, watercolors, watercolor brushes, containers for water, hole punch, scissors

Directions for One Set of Chaps:
1. Cut two sections from a grocery bag. Draw lines on the bottom of each section for fringe.
2. Use tape to reinforce the top edge of each section.
3. Halfway down each section, reinforce both sides with tape. Punch a hole in each reinforced area.
4. Fold the top of each section and tape several times to form a tube for the elastic band.
5. Have the children cut on the marker lines to make the fringe.
6. Let the children crumple up the paper bag sections and then lay the sections flat to paint with watercolors.
7. Once the paint has dried, insert elastic through the casing and tie the loose ends together to create the waistband.
8. Attach a pipe cleaner to each hole in the chaps. (These are the holes that are midway down the bags.)
9. Children pull on the chaps and fasten the pipe cleaners behind each leg.

21

Pioneer Shawl

Materials:
Butcher paper, scrap material, yarn, pipe cleaners, marker, masking tape or clear packing tape, glue, hole punch, scissors

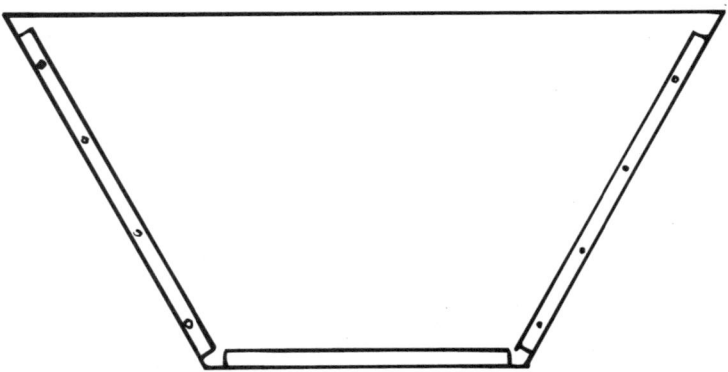

Directions:
1. Cut a trapezoidal shape out of butcher paper. (See above.) It should be large enough to form a shawl around a child's shoulders. Cut one per child.
2. Reinforce the edges along all sides with tape. Punch holes on two sides.
3. Cut small scraps of material.
4. For each shawl, cut several pieces of yarn (about 1 ft/.3 m).
5. Demonstrate how to make loop knot fringe by folding a piece of yarn in half, inserting the loop of the yarn through the hole, bringing the two loose ends of yarn through the loop, and pulling gently. Continue for each hole to complete the fringe, but do not put fringe through the two front holes. (These are for the pipe cleaners.)
6. Provide scraps of material for the children to glue onto the shawls.
7. Once the glue has dried, slide a pipe cleaner through each of the two front holes of the shawl. Bend one end of each pipe cleaner to hold it in place. The pipe cleaners are twisted together to secure the shawl.

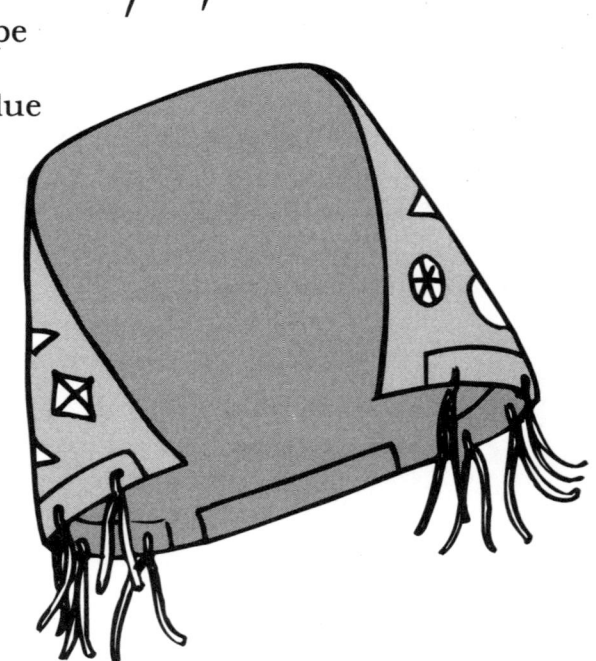

Pioneer Bonnet

Materials:
Construction paper, tissue paper, tempera paint, shallow tins for paint, cotton swabs, masking tape, pipe cleaners, hole punch, scissors

Directions:
1. Cut a 6-inch x 18-inch (15-cm x 45-cm) strip of construction paper. Make one per child.
2. Provide tempera paint and cotton swabs for children to use to decorate the hat brims.
3. Once the hat brims have dried, tape a piece of tissue paper to the inside of each brim.
4. On each hat, gather the top of the tissue paper and turn it inside. Secure with a pipe cleaner.
5. Reinforce the two ends of each hat brim with masking tape and punch a hole in each end.
6. Slide a pipe cleaner through each hole. Bend one end of each pipe cleaner to fasten it to the bonnet. The bonnet is secured under the chin with the pipe cleaners.

Note:
• Children can wear the bonnet with the Pioneer Shawl (p. 22).

Miner's Visor

Materials:
Sturdy paper, yellow or white construction paper, tempera paint, water, drinking straws (one per child), containers for paint, tape, spoons, marker, scissors

Directions:
1. On sturdy paper, draw a version of the miner's visor (shown on this page), and cut it out. (The hat should be large enough to fit around a child's head.) Make one per child.
2. Make circular patterns of headlamps on sturdy paper and cut them out. These become templates for the children to trace. Make several.
3. Provide watered-down tempera paint for the children to spoon in small amounts onto the hat. Children use straws to blow on the paint and form patterns.
4. Have the children trace the headlights on construction paper and cut them out.
5. Once the paint has dried, the children glue a headlight to the front of each hat brim.
6. Measure each child's miner's hat to his or her head and tape the loose ends together.
7. Fold the brim of the hat up.

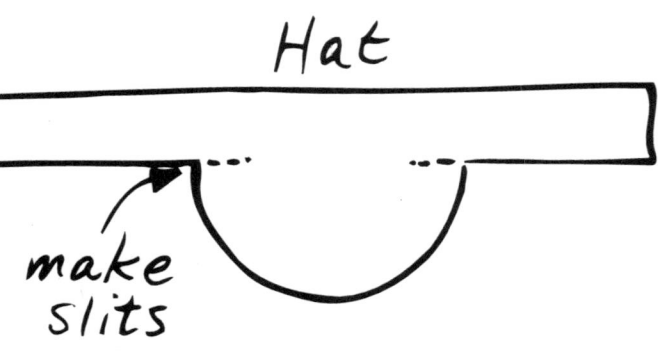

Note:
• The children can wear their miners' hats while panning for gold (p. 28).

Lantern

Materials:

Flame pattern (this page), large or small milk cartons (one per child), construction paper (red and orange), sturdy paper, markers, pipe cleaners, stapler, ice pick or screwdriver (for adult use only), sharp instrument for cutting (for adult use only)

Directions:

1. Rinse out the milk cartons and let them dry.
2. Staple the tops of the milk cartons closed.
3. Poke two holes opposite each other through the top of each milk carton.
4. Cut one rectangular opening on each side of each milk carton, and cut a slit on the bottom of each carton. (The slit should be large enough for the flame pattern to fit through.)
5. Trace the Flame pattern onto sturdy paper and cut it out. Make several for the children to use as templates.
6. Have the children trace the Flame Pattern onto the colored construction paper and cut it out.
7. Help the children insert a flame into the slit on the bottom of each lantern. Tape a portion of the flame to the bottom outside of the milk carton.
8. Have the children attach a pipe cleaner handle through the holes in the top of the cartons.

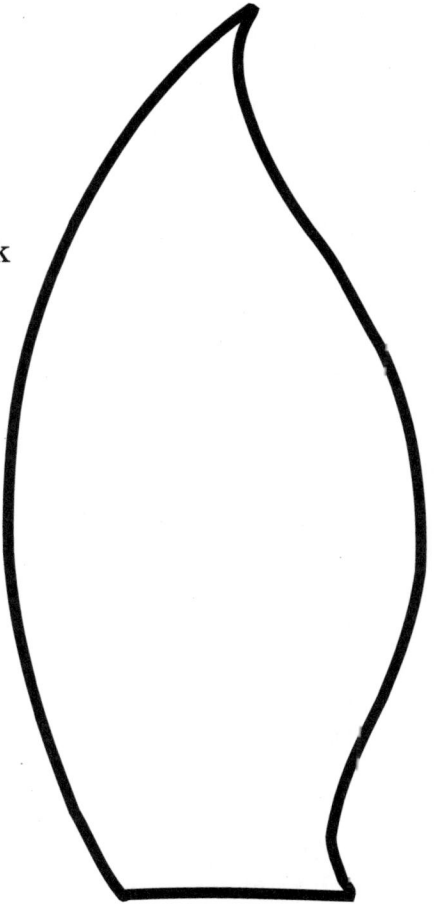

Wild West ©1999 Monday Morning Books, Inc.

Tie-Dyed Bedroll

Materials:
King-size pillowcase, fabric dye (for adult use only), pipe cleaners, large tub, long-handled wooden spoon, latex gloves (for adult use only)

Directions:
1. Have the children gather up fabric of the pillowcase and then twist the pipe cleaners around the fabric in several places.
2. Mix the fabric dye according to the directions.
3. Place the pillowcase in the dye and stir with a long-handled spoon. Don't let the fabric sit in the dye too long.
4. Wearing latex gloves, remove the pillowcase, squeeze out the excess liquid, and hang up to dry. Make sure to do this well away from the children. Wash the pillowcase in a regular washing machine and dry it thoroughly to ensure that the dye won't bleed if it gets wet.
5. Once the case has dried, let the children unwrap the pipe cleaners.
6. Children can use the bedroll in dramatic play. When they are finished, they can roll it up and secure it with a pipe cleaner.

Option:
• Experiment with more than one color of dye. Try dipping different parts of the pillowcase in different colors.

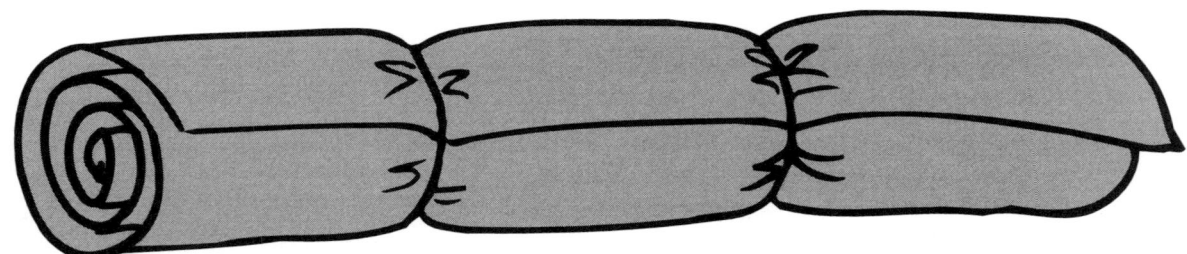

Cool Canteen

Materials:
Individual-sized plastic water bottles (one per child), yarn, clear packing tape, colored masking tape, stickers, scissors

Directions:
1. Cut yarn into 2-foot (60-cm) lengths. Make one per child.
2. Using clear packing tape, attach yarn to each water bottle for a shoulder strap.
3. Provide colored masking tape and stickers for the children to use to decorate their canteens.

Book Link:
• *Bubba the Cowboy Prince*
by Helen Ketterman (Scholastic)

Panning for Gold

Materials:
Aluminum pie pans, rocks and pebbles, gold spray paint (for adult use only), sand, large tub, water, newspaper

Directions:
1. Away from the children, spread the rocks and pebbles on newsprint and spray paint them gold. Let them dry, then turn them over and spray paint the other sides.
2. Place the sand and water in a large tub, making a mixture of more water than sand.
3. Mix the dried "gold nuggets" in the sand and water mixture.
4. Discuss the life of a miner with the children. Explain that people in the 1840s and 1850s headed for the west coast to get rich by panning for gold. Then provide aluminum pie pans for the children to use to pan for gold.

Facts to Share:
Gold miners often worked along creek beds and other bodies of water. They used pans to sift dirt and rocks from streams to find gold nuggets or particles. This was called "panning for gold."

Book Link:
• *Boom Town* by Sonia Levitin (Orchard)

Song Link:
• Teach the children "Clementine." It's about the daughter of a "miner 49er!"

Campfire Ring

Materials:
Lunch-sized paper bags, cardboard tubes (from paper towels and toilet tissue), tissue paper (red and orange), newspaper or Styrofoam pieces, used and dried coffee grounds, shallow trays for coffee grounds, tempera paint (black and white), glue, shallow tins for paint and glue, paintbrushes, masking tape

Directions:
1. Have the children stuff the paper bags with crumpled newspaper or Styrofoam pieces.
2. Tape the bags closed.
3. Let the children mix black and white tempera paint together to make gray paint. Have them paint the paper bags gray. (These resemble rocks.)
4. Have the children paint glue on the tubes and roll the tubes in the coffee grounds.
5. Once the glue has dried, have the children stuff tissue paper into the ends of the tubes for flames.
6. Make a fire ring from the paper bag rocks and place the "burning logs" in the center.

Note:
• Use the Campfire Ring with the Cooking Pots and Pans (p. 30) and Cooking Stand (p. 31).

Option:
• Teach the children campfire songs.

     Wild West ©1999 Monday Morning Books, Inc.

Cooking Pots and Pans

Materials:
Masking tape, circular cardboard ice cream containers with lids, tongue depressors, aluminum foil, pipe cleaners, sharp instrument for cutting (for adult use only)

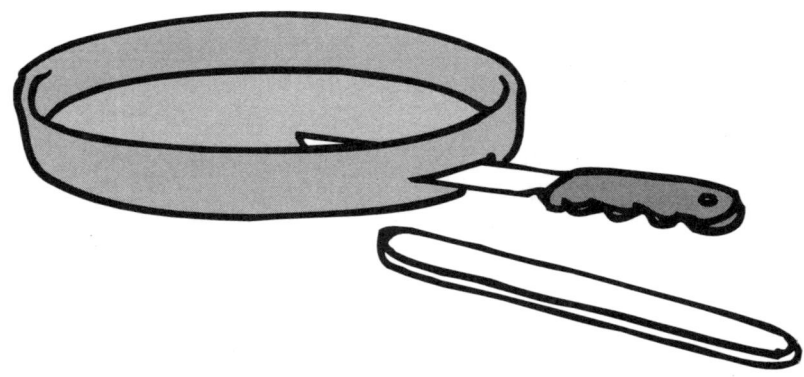

Directions:
1. Have the children wrap the ice cream containers and lids with aluminum foil. (They should wrap the containers and lids separately.)
2. Poke a hole on two opposite sides of each ice cream container. Have the children attach pipe cleaners for handles.
3. Cut a slit in one side of the ice cream container lids. Children insert a tongue depressor through the slit and tape it to the inside of the lid.

Facts to Share:
During pioneer times, meals generally included bread, bacon, dried beans, salt pork, or flapjacks. Iron pots were used to cook beans, stews, and other foods. Pancakes were cooked in iron skillets.

Cooking Stand

Materials:
Three yardsticks or three 3-foot (1-m) long dowels, black tempera paint, shallow tins for paint, paintbrushes, wire coat hanger, masking tape, sharp instrument for cutting (for adult use only), wire cutter (for adult use only)

Directions:
1. Cut the wire coat hanger according to the diagram.

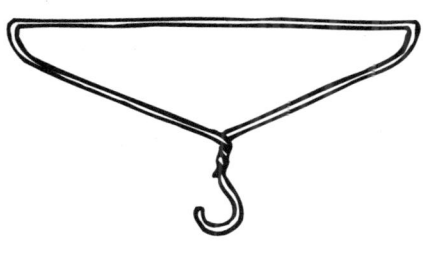 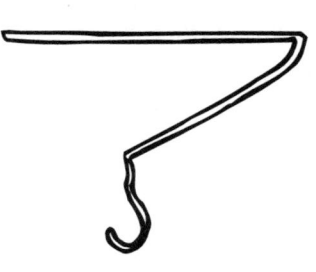 

2. Tape yardsticks or dowels into a tripod.
3. Provide tempera paint for the children to use to paint the cooking stand.
4. Once the paint has dried, wrap the cut section of the coat hanger around the neck of the cooking stand. Bend the hook to hang between the legs of the stand. (Wrap all exposed ends of the wire with masking tape.)

Note:
• Place a Cooking Pot (p. 30) on the hook and put over the Campfire Ring.

Book Link:
• *The Carrot Seed* by Ruth Krauss (Harper & Row)

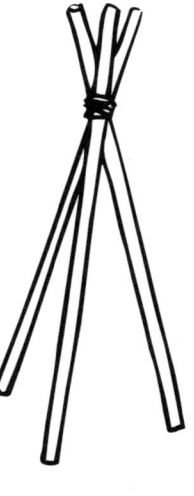

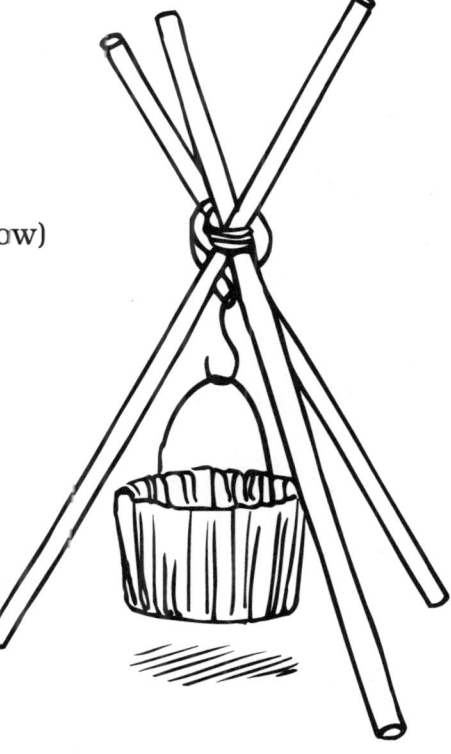

Western Town

Materials:
Assorted boxes (computer paper, cereal, facial tissue), construction paper (in assorted colors), sturdy paper, Popsicle sticks, markers and crayons, glue and paste, scissors, picture books about towns in the Wild West

Directions:
1. Show the children pictures of western towns.
2. Give the children their choices of boxes to use to create buildings for a western town. Suggest that they might create banks, stores, houses, hotels, and schools.
3. Provide Popsicle sticks for the children to glue onto strips of sturdy paper to make wooden sidewalks.

Note:
• Use the Western Town with the Miniature Stagecoach (p. 33).

Miniature Stagecoach

Materials:

Square facial tissue box (one per child), metal juice lids (four per child), brads, red tissue paper, liquid starch, containers for starch, paintbrushes, marker, scissors, ice pick or screwdriver (for adult use only)

Directions:

1. Cut a door with a window on one side of each box. Cut windows on all sides of each of the boxes.

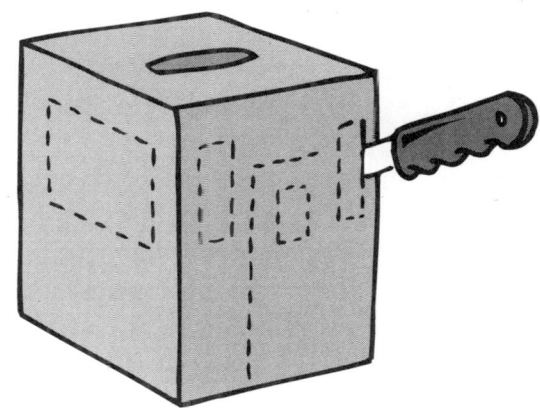

2. Punch two holes on two opposite sides for the wheels.
3. Punch one hole in each juice lid with an ice pick or screwdriver. Attach wheels to the boxes with brads.
4. Provide tissue paper and starch for the children to use to cover the stagecoaches.

Note:

• Use the Stagecoach with the Western Town (p. 32), the Popsicle Stick Horse (p. 34), and the Stagecoach Luggage (p. 36).

Book Link:

• *Westward Ho, Carlotta!* by Candace Fleming (Atheneum)

Popsicle Stick Horse

Materials:
Horse Head pattern (p. 35), Playdough recipe (p. 35), sturdy paper or old file folders, pipe cleaners, Popsicle sticks, markers, crayons, colored pencils, scissors

Directions:
1. Make the playdough with the children, using caution when adding the boiling water.
2. Cut pipe cleaners in half.
3. Trace the Horse Head pattern onto sturdy paper. Make one per child.
4. Have the children cut out the Horse Heads and color them and the Popsicle sticks with crayons, markers, or colored pencils.
5. Give each child a ball of playdough to roll into an oblong shape.
6. Have the children stick four Popsicle sticks into their playdough balls for legs. They can also add the horse heads and the pipe cleaner tails.

Note:
• Use the Popsicle Stick Horse with the Miniature Stage Coach (p. 33).

Playdough Recipe

Ingredients:
4 cups (1 kilogram) flour
2 cups (.5 kilogram) salt
8 tsp. (40 grams) cream of tartar
10 tsp. (50 ml.) vegetable oil
4 cups (1 liter) boiling water
Food coloring (desired color)

Directions:
1. Combine the first four ingredients in a large bowl.
2. Add food coloring to the boiling water. (Do this away from the children!)
3. Pour the water into the dry ingredients and mix.
4. Remove the dough from the bowl and knead on a floured surface.

35

Stagecoach Luggage

Materials:
Toothpick boxes (or other small boxes; one per child), pipe cleaners, tempera paint, shallow tins for paint, paintbrushes or cotton swabs, scissors

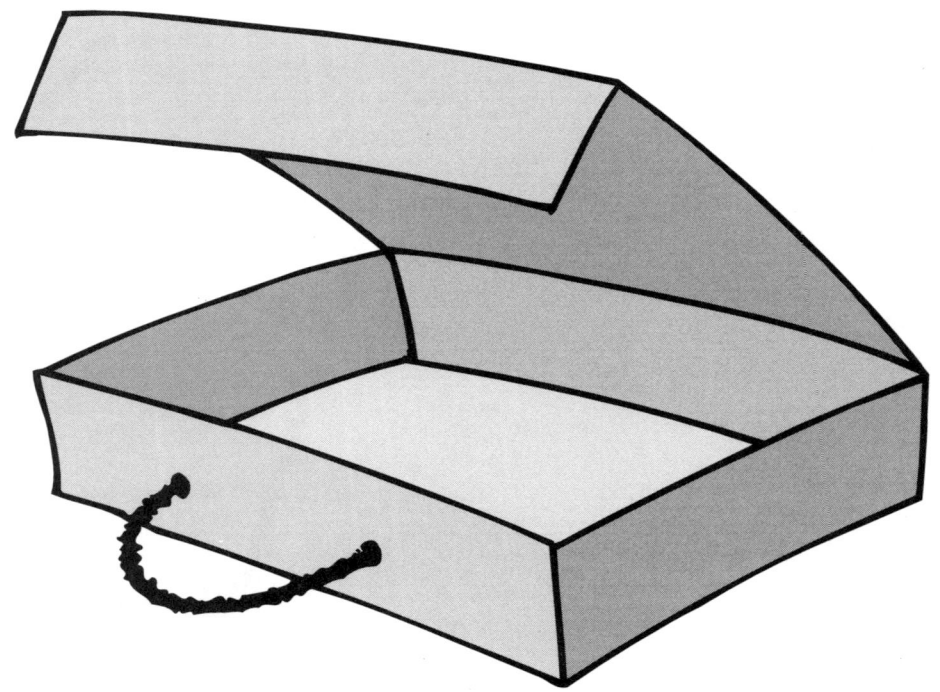

Directions:
1. Provide tempera paint for the children to use to paint the toothpick boxes.
2. Once the paint has dried, poke two small holes in one side of each box and attach pipe cleaner handles.

Note:
• Children can use the Stagecoach Luggage with the Miniature Stagecoach (p. 33) and the Miniature Pioneers (p. 38).

Oatmeal Box Wagon Train

Materials:
Oatmeal boxes (one per child), rectangular tissue boxes (one per child), brown grocery bags, cloth scraps, scissors, crayons, poster board, glue, jar lids

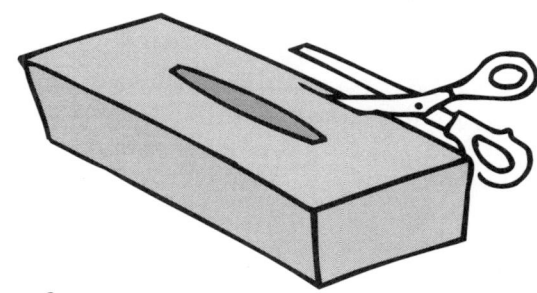

Directions:
1. Cut the top side off of each tissue box.
2. Show the children how to assemble the tissue boxes and the oatmeal boxes. Put glue on the side of an oatmeal box, then set it glue-side down inside the tissue box.
3. Have each child trace a jar lid four times onto construction paper and cut them out for wheels.
4. Have the children glue the wheels to the sides of the tissue boxes.
5. Children can cover their oatmeal boxes with cloth scraps to make wagon covers.
6. Let the children place their wagons in a long row to make a wagon train.

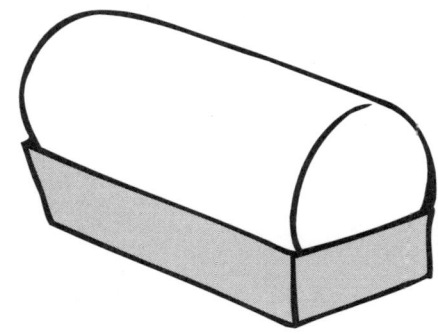

Note:
• Children can use Popsicle Stick Horses (p. 34) to draw the Oatmeal Box Wagons.

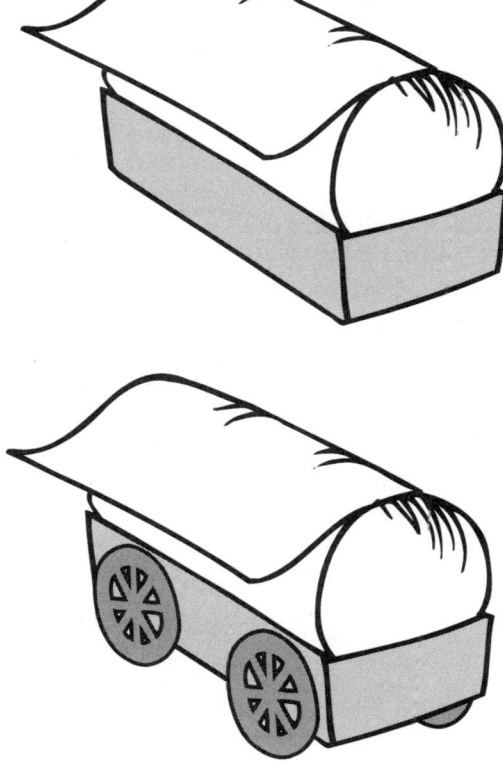

Wild West ©1999 Monday Morning Books, Inc.

Miniature Pioneers

Materials:
Pioneer Clothing patterns (pp. 39-40), individual-sized plastic juice containers without lids (one per child), Styrofoam balls, colored construction paper, yarn (black, brown, red, and yellow), markers, glue sticks, scissors, markers

Directions:
1. Rinse out the juice containers and let them dry.
2. Cut the yarn into small pieces.
3. Trace the Pioneer Clothing patterns onto colored construction paper. Make one set of clothing per child.
4. Have the children attach a Styrofoam ball to a juice container by pushing the ball on the opening of the juice container. (Help the children who need it.)
5. Have the children use markers to draw facial features on the Styrofoam balls.
6. Give each child a set of clothing to cut out and attach to the miniature pioneers using glue sticks.
7. The children can glue the yarn to their dolls for hair.

Book Link:
• *Cowboy Baby* by Sue Heap (Candlewick)

Pioneer Clothing

Pioneer Clothing

Cooking Pot Color Match

Materials:

Cooking Stand Game Board (pp. 42-43), Cooking Pots (p. 44), colored markers or pencils (in rainbow colors), clear contact paper, scissors, clear tape

Directions:

1. Duplicate a copy of the game board pattern, and attach the two halves using tape.
2. Color each pot on the game board using the correct color.
3. Laminate the game board or cover with clear contact paper.
4. Duplicate the game cards, color each pot using the correct color, and cut apart. Laminate and cut apart again, leaving a thin laminate border to prevent peeling.
5. Children match the colored pots on the cards to the correct pots on the game board.

Option

• Make a game set for each child. Let the children glue the pots to the correct cooking stands on the game boards.

Wild West ©1999 Monday Morning Books, Inc.

Cooking Stand Game Board

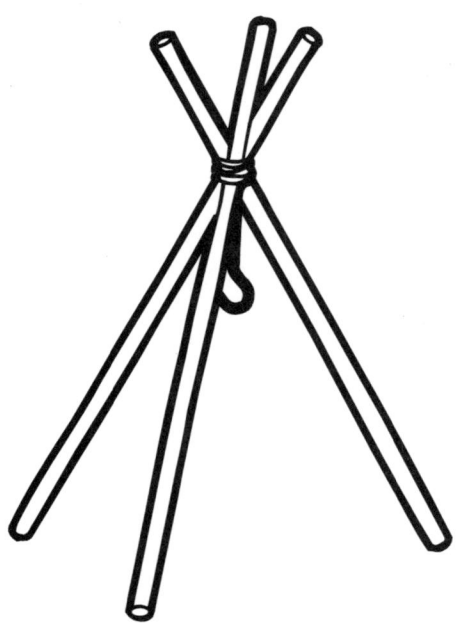

green

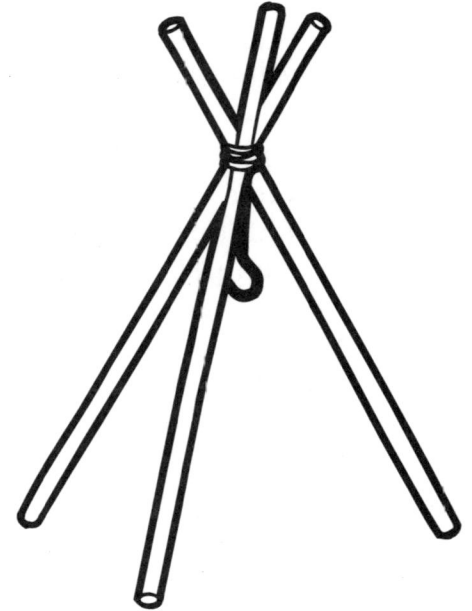

blue

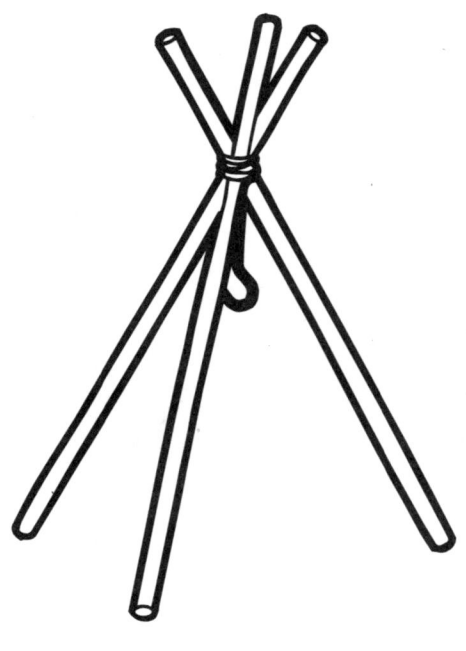

purple

Cooking Stand Game Board

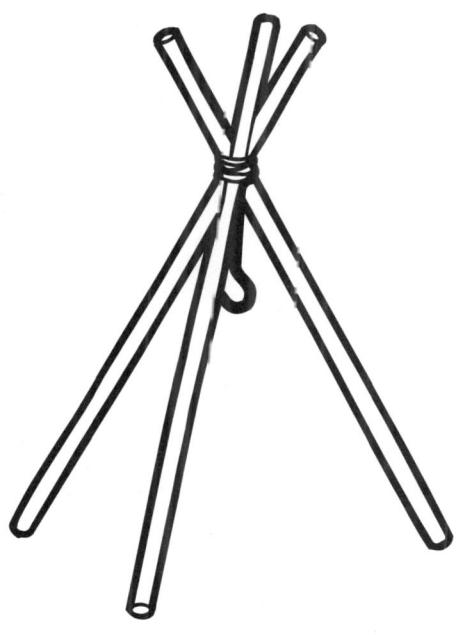

red

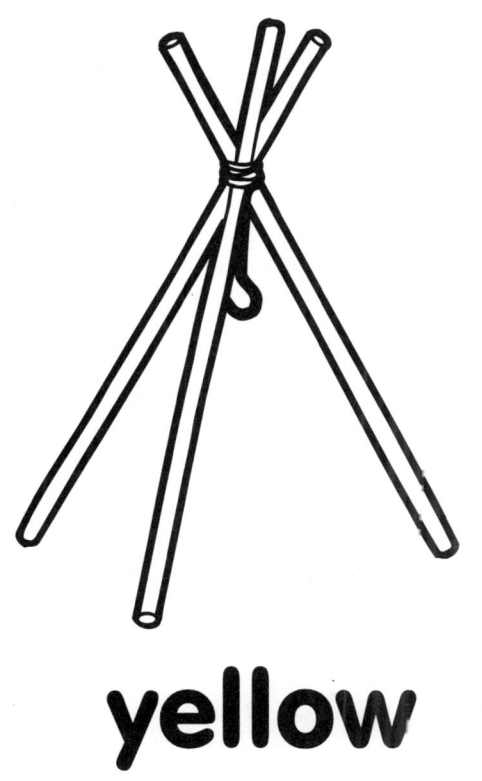

yellow

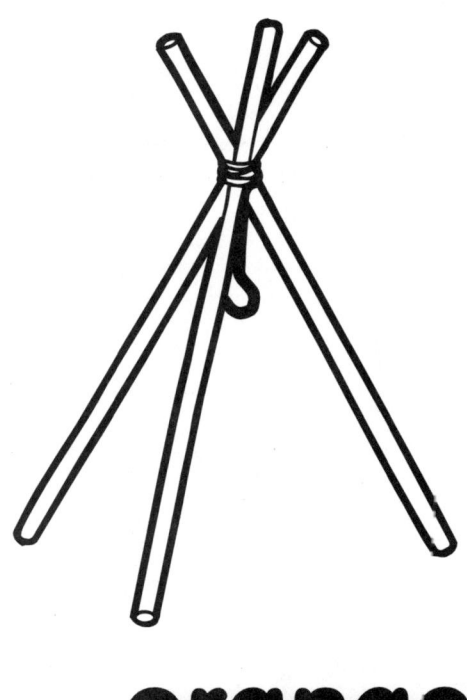

orange

Cooking Pots

red

purple

orange

blue

yellow

green

Stagecoach Number Match

Materials:
Stagecoach Journey (p. 46), crayons or markers, self-sticking dots

Directions:
1. Duplicate a copy of the Stagecoach Journey for each child.
2. Write the numerals from one to nine on the self-sticking dots. Make a set of stickers for each child.
3. Have the children match the numerals to the corresponding dots on the pattern.
4. Provide crayons or markers for the children to use to color their pictures.

Options:
• If self-sticking dots are not available, cut circles from construction paper and number these. Children can glue the circles to the patterns.
• Write the numbers out of order on the dots.
• For more advanced children, white-out the dots on the pattern before duplicating it.
Have the children write the numbers from one to nine in the circles.

Wild West ©1999 Monday Morning Books, Inc.

Stagecoach Journey

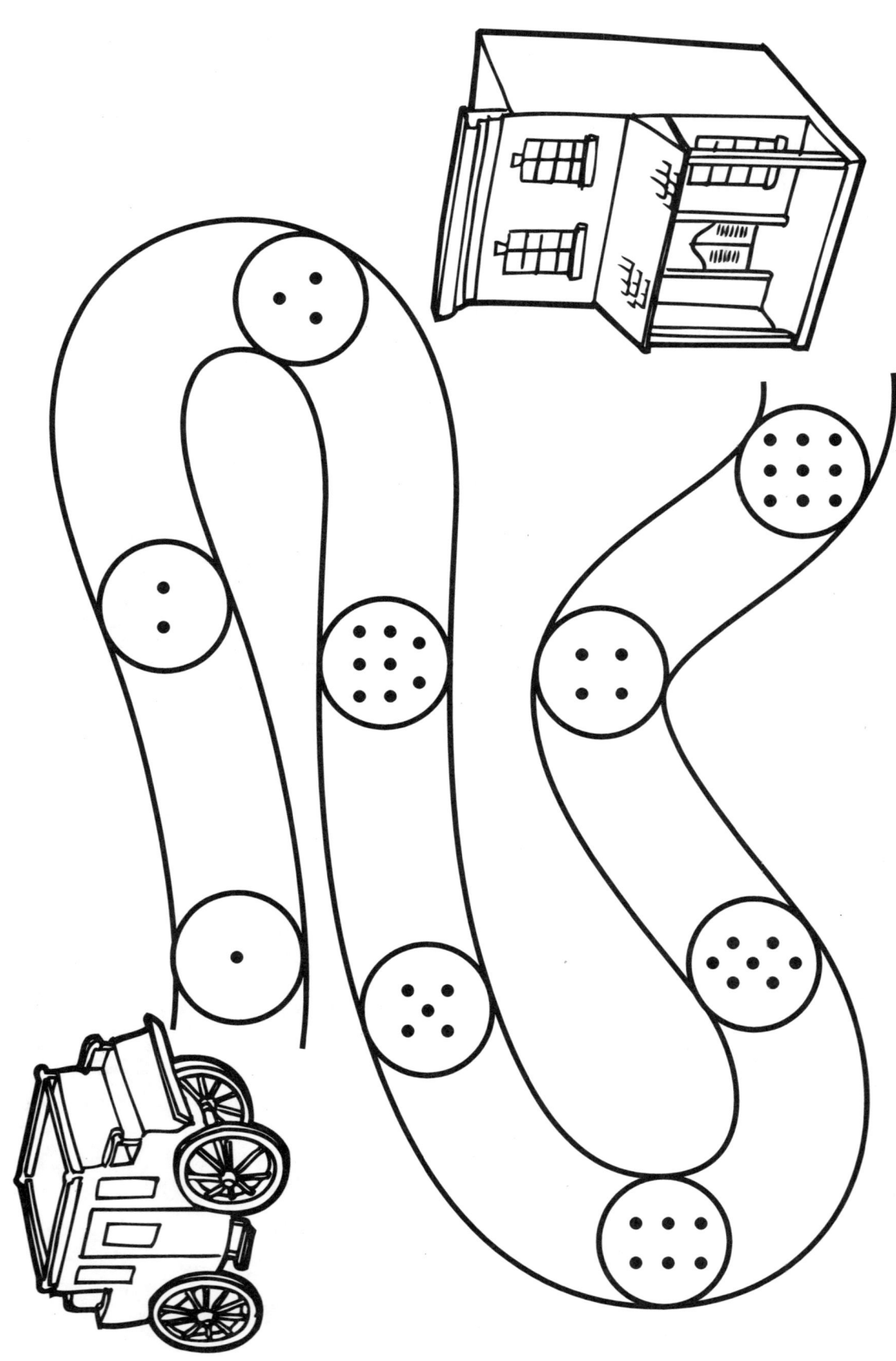

Wild West Memory Match

Materials:
Wild West Patterns (p. 48), colored
markers, scissors, clear
contact paper

Directions:
1. Duplicate the Wild West Patterns twice, color, cut apart,
cover with contact paper or laminate, and cut out again.
(Leave a thin laminate border to prevent peeling.)
2. Shuffle the cards and spread them face down on a table.
3. Demonstrate how to play the game. The object is to
match the Wild West Patterns by turning the cards over two
at a time. If a match is made, the cards remain face up and
the child takes another turn. If a match is not made, the
cards are turned over and the next child takes a turn. The
game continues until all cards are face up.

Options:
• Introduce the game by leaving the shuffled cards face up
and having the children simply match the Wild West
Patterns together.
• Enlarge and decorate these patterns, and use them to
decorate bulletin boards during this unit.

Wild West Patterns